SWAG

6 Battle Tested Strategies
to Build and Protect Your Confidence

MICHEAL J. BURT

PREMISE OF THE BOOK

Confidence is the one thing that affects everything.

It is the memory of success and the ammunition one needs to manifest his or her thoughts into reality.

Confidence can be built, maintained, and protected systematically.

For far too long, however, a lack of confidence has been the great disabler of millions of talented people who have listened to others in their pasts, saw their lives as failures, or relied on the false opinions of others for their sense of self-worth and value.

For something so important and so vital to long-term success, one would think that courses on confidence would be required for every middle school, high school, college, and trade school curriculum in America. Unfortunately, no such course of study exists.

This lack of education in this key area sets people up to fail later in life ending in under-realized potential, failed marriages, dysfunctional relationships, under-performing teams, and dreams that never materialize.

This little book serves as the perfect antidote for such negative outcomes, outlining six battle-tested strategies to build and protect your greatest asset—confidence—or what author Micheal Burt prefers to refer to as "SWAG."

As a former women's basketball coach, Burt saw how confidence affected virtually every player on every team. When he transitioned to coaching and developing adults, he saw how this single enabler or disabler touched everyone with whom he came in contact.

Many people know they need more SWAG and can see how it is directly attached to their potential—and yet they have no idea what it is, what erodes it, how to build it, or how to protect it! Entrepreneurs and small business owners in particular often allow outside factors such as market conditions, the economy, local and national politics, or competition to negatively affect their SWAG.

In the following pages, Coach Burt tackles this subject of confidence head on and provides clear and easy-to-understand instruction on how people can protect their greatest asset. From high school students to corporate CEO's, this little book is sure to make a huge difference in how people can evolve into what they envision they can become when they utilize their greatest tool—SWAG!

In this book, Coach Burt explores the following battle-tested strategies to build and protect SWAG:
1. What is SWAG and how is it tied to success?
2. What erodes SWAG and how you can get it back?
3. What builds SWAG and enables your bigger future?
4. What maintains and protects SWAG once it has been attained?
5. How can you protect the SWAG of your business?
6. What is the difference between SWAG, arrogance, and boldness?

Who can benefit from these lessons?
• Individuals who need SWAG to produce: salespeople, leaders, athletes, coaches, actors, entrepreneurs, small business leaders, and managers;
• Parents who wish to instill SWAG in their children;
• Education systems that realize the need to teach courses on SWAG as an integral part of life preparation.

TABLE OF CONTENTS:

ACKNOWLEDGEMENTS

It takes a village to build confidence in young people so it is implanted in their hearts and minds. Instilling SWAG is about affirming and validating the worth and potential in another in such a clear way that they begin to see it in themselves.

Thank you to my mother for affirming that I could become whatever I wanted to be in life and putting me in positions to find my voice, which led to the knowledge and confidence that I was on the "right bus" in life.

Thank you to the coaches who told me at an early age that I would and could become a great coach someday. You inspired me to manifest my destiny.

Thank you to my editing and design team of Mitzi Brandon, Drew Ruble, and Sherry Wiser George, who take my ideas and turn them into reality. The back stage isn't always glamorous but it makes the front stage possible.

Thank you to my beautiful daughter, Michella Grace, for inspiring me to create a new sense of urgency in life, live from a grander vision, and allow me to be your biggest fan as you fulfill your Dharma some day.

Finally, thank you to Michella's beautiful mother, Natalie, who has inspired so much SWAG in both myself and our daughter. I will always be grateful for the blessing of having you in my life.

Other Books by Coach Micheal Burt:

Changing Lives through Coaching	*Small Towns Big Dreams*
The Inspirational Leader	*Person of Interest*
This Ain't No Practice Life	*The Intangibles*
The Anatomy of Winning	*Zebras and Cheetahs*

FOREWORD

On a cold winter night last February, I received a call from a dear friend from my high school days. He was dejected. His second marriage was falling apart, his work wasn't fulfilling him, and he knew in his core that he was drastically under-utilizing the potential and talent he had been given in life. He was calling for help and direction.

I listened for a while to see if I could diagnose his scenario through a filter I commonly use with anyone seeking my guidance. I look at all parts of a person's nature by using what's called "The Whole Person Theory" that says people are made up of four parts:

First, a body, which equates to skill and discipline. Second, a mind, which equates to knowledge and expertise. Next, a heart, which equates to desire and passion…

Then I reach the fourth part, confidence, which equates to the spirit and the ability to have an internal knowing that one can manifest what he or she sees in their mind or can bounce back from unwanted outcomes.

It was obvious to me what my friend had lost: his SWAG!

SWAG is a new age slang term for confidence; but it's more than just saying confidence—it's SWAGGER. It's belief. It's mindset. It's effort. It's the way you walk. It's the way you talk. It's your total approach to "owning" the life you envision for yourself in your mind and a total confidence that you can and will bounce back from any unwanted scenarios in life.

SWAG is the one thing that affects everything. It is the great enabler or the great disabler. It trumps all the negative noise we hear from others and the world about how we should conform and fit in vs. stand out and dominate.

I stopped the conversation midway through and said, "I know exactly what you need." He replied, "What is that?" I said, "You need your SWAG back." I then proceeded to remind him of how popular he was in high school, how he was voted "Most Likely to Succeed," how he was a former sports star, and how his life was so full of promise. I reminded him of the confidence he used to display but had somehow lost along his journey. From my perspective, it was time for him to get that SWAG back. If not, we would be having this conversation over and over again while the precious depreciating asset of time slipped way.

I continued the conversation. "I'm glad you came to me because I specialize in instilling SWAG in people," I said. "Because I understand one thing—when you're low on SWAG, you can borrow from somebody else."

Just as I frequently borrow from my buddy, Grant Cardone (author of *The 10X Rule*), my dejected high school buddy could now borrow from me.

Think of SWAG as momentum, possibility, movement in a positive direction, focus, belief, and an attitude of "I will conquer" vs. "I cannot win."

The original title of this book was *A Course in Confidence*. However, after my conversation with my friend, I knew the title didn't have enough SWAG to it.

I'm looking for edge. I'm looking to wake up the dead. I'm looking to implant and install a chip in people that helps them ignite their dreams, conquer their fears, and go to places they have never gone before.

I know one thing for certain. Once SWAG is lost, you are on the wrong side of momentum and are headed in the wrong direction. I also know that you can get SWAG back. It's just a matter of shifting that momentum in a new direction.

Thank you for coming to the SWAG doctor. When you're done reading this book, you'll have all the SWAG you need. Once you discover it, or unearth it, don't ever give it up again. Don't ever let a person or group of people steal it from you or cause it to shrink. And never, I mean never, let anything from your past reach up and steal the future of your SWAG.

INTRODUCTION

I looked at my schedule of pre-planned talks that I was giving all over the country and saw this: "A Course in Confidence: Manifesting Your Bigger Future," which I was to deliver the following week in Jackson, Tennessee. As I do with all of my talks, I wrote an outline on the topic to help guide my thinking:

1. What is confidence and why does it seem so elusive to so many?
2. What erodes or destroys confidence in people?
3. How can we build confidence?
4. How can we maintain and protect it once it is built?
5. How can we protect the confidence of our business?

Outline in hand, I went to Jackson to test drive the new talk on a group of wealth advisors I had been working with for more than two years. Month after month, I had shared some topic with this group and they always seemed to "get" them. In fact, many had begun to produce at all new levels.

On this day, they honed in like never before. Could it be that I had found a universal topic that would interest everyone? Could it be that confidence, or, as I like to call it "SWAG" is the ONE THING that affects everything? Could it be that this topic of SWAG either propels us to great success or shackles our minds and hearts to a state of, well, mediocrity?

The next day at a different location in middle Tennessee, I repeated the talk. One of the participants came up afterwards and said, "This was the best talk you have ever given." Bingo. I knew I was on to something.

When I was a high school basketball coach, I would hear parents say to their children, "You need more confidence because you've got loads of potential." The problem, though, was that no one ever explained to their children what this confidence or SWAG was and how to reach the potential they believed existed!

The same is true of adults. They too need more SWAG because they too have greater potential—they just need someone to explain what SWAG is, how it can be activated, and how it can be protected against the barrage of images, words, and thoughts that seek to destroy it daily.

I believe SWAG is either the great enabler of success or the great disabler of success. It either propels a person forward to a brighter future or the lack of it is holding them back from the same. It is either the ammunition you need to succeed or the hindrance that is keeping you from advancing confidently in the direction of your dreams.

I also believe that great coaches and mentors across the globe help us build, maintain, and protect our SWAG. They also help us get it back when we've lost it. As such, this book is for every person, young or old, who has potential and needs the ammunition to make their dreams a reality. They need SWAG.

This book is also for the person who already has SWAG but wants to protect, maintain, and grow it because they know it is integral to their bigger futures.

Every successful person in the world has this ingredient of SWAG embedded in their daily actions and interactions. By contrast, a life without SWAG is a life of quiet desperation, of never trying, of being controlled by the opinions of others, and of living in the past.

We don't want that life. We want the special one we envision. The only thing stopping us from having it is the one thing that affects everything—SWAG!

Every great coach challenges their players to do three things:
1. Conduct the conversations you hesitate to have or don't want to have.
2. Do the things you are avoiding and flat-out do not want to do.
3. Become the person you know that you can be but too often think you can never become.

Let me help you achieve those changes with this book. Let me share with you the six battle-tested strategies to build and protect your greatest asset—SWAG!

Micheal

Coach Micheal Burt
St. Thomas, U.S. Virgin Islands

CHAPTER 1:
THE BATTLEFIELD
What is SWAG and how do we obtain it?

When I think about confidence, I go back to my senior year of high school and the last basketball game I played in my career. I was the point guard, and we were playing Jackson County in a district tournament game.

As the game went on, my performance got worse. I remember my coach, Alan Bush, saying to me, "Burt, what is wrong with you? You have turned the ball over six times in this game."

I didn't know what to say; but looking back on that dreadful game (which we eventually lost) I now know what happened. I totally lost my confidence and it affected everything I was doing.

We spend a lot of time telling young people and adults that they "just need more confidence" but not a lot of time telling them what confidence is or where they can get some. We're perceptive enough to know the lack of it when we see it in others and smart enough to know that all successful people have it. However, despite those keen observations, there continues to be exponentially more people who lack confidence than possess it.

No wonder successful people who possess SWAG stand out so much, are willing to take risks, and benefit the most from it—not to mention why so many people mistake SWAG for arrogance. Just like poor people who think all rich people are evil, or those who never win and are jealous of those who always win, they know the secret ingredient that is holding them back is locked up in one word: SWAG!

SWAG is:

- confidence to believe
- confidence to act
- confidence to bounce back
- confidence to manifest your destiny
- confidence to strive and reach for your bigger future
- confidence to see opposition as opportunity
- confidence to transform negative situations into positive ones
- confidence to build the resilience it takes to be extraordinary
- confidence to stand out vs. fit in
- confidence to get better vs. just go along and get along
- confidence to swim upstream when it's so much easier to float downstream
- confidence to take the high road when the low road is a much easier ride
- confidence to make a stand about who you are and what you believe in as opposed to laying down
- confidence to know what you are doing really matters and that your life counts

Don't hate the players, just hate the game. And this game is about SWAG. So what is it, and where can I get some?

I was a junior in college when I was fortunate enough to forge a relationship with a wonderful sports psychologist named Dr. Aaron Solomon. A former head baseball coach and major league pitcher, Dr. Solomon recognized something in me, affirmed my worth and value, and told me I would become something special one day.

He also taught me the best definition I had ever heard of SWAG. In his words, he said confidence is the "memory of success." I began sharing that concept with people all over the world until finally someone in one of my audiences pushed back and said, "Well, what if we never have any success? How then can we become confident?"

It was a great question. I then replied, "Success is the continued expansion of happiness and the progressive realization of worthy goals." Their response? "Okay, but how do we obtain that?"

My answer has become the foundation of my focus on living life with SWAG. We have success through consistent, repetitive, ongoing, systematic practice. Just like anything else in life, our confidence is tied to our whole person—meaning our body, our mind, our heart, and our spirit. Each of these parts produce four needs, four capacities, and four intelligences:

• Body, or Skills
• Mind, or Knowledge
• Heart, or Effort
• Spirit, or Confidence—SWAG

The better the skill you have, the more confident you will be. The more knowledge you have, the more confident you will be. The more effort you put into something, the more confident you will be. Each of these capacities or intelligences feeds confidence.

When you are lacking in knowledge, skill, or desire, you will be lacking in confidence or belief. The key is to get diligently to work practicing consistent, ongoing, systematic effort in a specific field. As you grow your knowledge, skills, and desire in an area, you will begin to feel more confident. Couple these ingredients with feedback from the market (i.e. a coach, buyers, friends, loved ones, fans, etc. who notice your effort and improvement) and you will have both internal markers for confidence (knowledge, skills, desire) and external markers for confidence (positive feedback from the market and others).

How does this apply to you?

No matter what you want to do with your life, incorporating these capacities or intelligences into your approach will get you there. Do you want to be a writer? Write a blog everyday on a different subject. Study the people who write the best blogs in your chosen space and who are world class. Read all of their material, immerse yourself into their work, and write every day. Over time, if you have the talent, you will begin to feel confident. You will begin to feel SWAG. The market will reward you with fans, money, love, repute, referrals, and positive affirmations. This, in turn, will build more SWAG!

Most people I work with who lack confidence also lack knowledge, effort, and desire. They don't try; therefore, they don't really know if they are capable of something or not. They assume it will be too hard and begin to make mistakes even before giving it a clear shot.

Do not be one of these people. Once you try enough things, you will begin to see what builds your SWAG and what erodes it. You will develop the resilience and begin to understand that failing at something actually builds and re-enforces confidence. Soon you can deduct where your talent lies, and you can align your time, energy, resources, and creativity with only those things that fit with your talents and gifts.

Dr. Solomon was right on the money. Confidence is the memory of success, and success only happens when we build key areas in a consistent and systematic way versus a random and sporadic one. Just like having a gym membership will not make you confident about your body if you don't use it, a failure to grow your knowledge, skills, desire, or confidence in the key areas you love will begin to decay or erode your SWAG. Practice sounds boring, but it's where the good stuff happens and the deep muscles really grow.

In the next chapter, we will look at what erodes your SWAG (now that you know exactly what it is!) When people tell you that you need confidence, what they are really saying is that you need to taste some success and that you need to get to work practicing hard in your key area.

CHAPTER 2:
BATTLE SCARS

There is no transformation without opposition. What will erode my SWAG?

Dan Sullivan, founder of *The Strategic Coach*® once said, "There is no transformation where there is no opposition." It is the opposition or resistance in life that offers the raw materials for transformation.

Your own mind many times provides the obstacles to SWAG because it listens to the past, other people, the "noise," and it tells you all of the reasons you will never be confident and never be great.

I have found that there are seven things that will erode your confidence. In this chapter, we first identify the obstacles to SWAG so we can move them out of the way and get to how we build, maintain, and protect it.

Remember, the opposition provides the raw materials for the transformation to take place. Don't let adversity limit or erode your SWAG but rather see it as the "seeds of greatness."

Eroding SWAG Enemy No. 1: The past will erode your confidence

If there is one big thing that will erode a person's confidence, it is living in the past—past failures, past problems, past successes, and past shortcomings.

The past is finite. It's fixed. By contrast, the future is infinite. It's unlimited to the abundantly-minded person.

Well-being expert Deepak Chopra once said, "Depressed people live in the past. Anxious people live in the future. Peaceful people live in the present."

Many people I meet who are not confident have allowed someone in their past to erode their confidence. They sold them a bill of goods and for some reason they bought it, most likely because they were low on SWAG.

Never let your past hold your future hostage. Here are some ways the past can tear down your confidence if you choose to live there.

• You had a failure in your past that you let define you.
• You had a person in your past that you let destroy you.
• You had some unexpected success in your past that you are still living in.

If you choose to listen to your memories and the negative feelings attached to them, know this—they make lousy leaders. Your memory will replay the past over and over again. Your memory will tell you that you are who you *used* to be, not who you are now or who you are going to be.

You will also have people who judge you based on your past—your past reputation, your past transgressions, or your past failures. Scarcity-minded people will define you in ways that are non-threatening to them. In essence, they will seek to make you look smaller by making themselves look bigger.

Don't let them define you. Don't let your past erode your future SWAG. You need a new tape playing in your head that can erase your past transgressions that are keeping you from being confident today.

I meet people every day who are still letting some past situation, relationship, or struggle affect every single decision they make today and will make tomorrow. It sabotages all of their healthy confidence and sabotages the SWAG extended to them by others.

Remember Chopra's saying, "Depressed people live in the past. Peaceful people live in the present?" We want to be peaceful and confident.

Leave the past in the past and learn to leverage the negative memory as a lighting bolt to a much bigger future.

Eroding SWAG Enemy No. 2: Being dependent on the good opinion of others

Abraham Maslow, the father of the self-actualization theory, said there are several core traits of a self-actualized person, one who reaches and actualizes his or her deepest human potential. One of those traits is being "independent of the good opinion of others."

If all of your SWAG is dependent on what other people think of you, then your SWAG will be eroded every time another person doesn't like your work, makes a dig about your performance, offers an unsavory opinion of you, or gives you negative feedback.

We can't disempower our own selves and allow the weaknesses of others to control us. When we give our confidence up to others, though, that is exactly what we are doing.

Think of SWAG as an internal knowing that you can manifest something in your life.

From an early age, deep emotional cancers of comparing, competing, complaining, criticizing, and contending are hardwired into people. Because of this scarcity mindset, others are taught that they are in competition for success, praise, attention, and recognition. This leads to jealously, small-minded thinking, and a mindset that says there is only so much good to go around.

Nothing could be further from the truth. If you went to the ocean to get water, you could get a teaspoon or a twenty-gallon bucket. The ocean doesn't care because the water is infinite. It's everywhere like the air that we breath.

SWAG is the ammunition you need to tackle new tasks, get off the bench, overcome opposition, and see an idea through to its logical conclusion, and only when you say it's not yours does it become vulnerable.

Take feedback from others as "feed-forward." Know that it is just their opinion, and that doesn't make it right or wrong.

Here's a motto I live by: "Some will buy what I'm selling. Some won't buy what I'm selling. SO WHAT? I just keep on moving."

Eroding SWAG Enemy No. 3: Not paying the price and knowing it

SWAG always comes from preparation. It never comes from winging it.

Those who pay the price in preparation, knowledge, skills, and effort will always be more confident than those who have not. In a sense, you have to know that you have "paid the price" to enjoy the success that is on its way.

Financial guru Dave Ramsey always says that you will have to "live like nobody else so that one day you can live like nobody else."

Confidence is the memory of success. Success is the expansion of happiness and the progressive realization of worthy goals. We have success with a consistent formula:

Success = Consistency + Ongoing + Repetitive + Systematic Practice.

This process will require discipline, and discipline is a derivative of the word "disciple," which is where you give yourself to a person or cause you believe in. I ask people, "Do you believe in your own future?" They all say yes. I then ask, "Where does your future reside?" The correct answer is that it resides in one place—your imagination. No one else can see what's in your mind. If you don't manifest what is in your mind, it's nobody's fault but your own because no one else can see your imagination.

Paying the price to build SWAG means that you will do whatever it takes to grow yourself in these areas:

- the mind—grow your knowledge to become the foremost expert in a specific field.
- the body—pay the price to be in the best shape you have ever been in. Eat right, sleep right, and exercise right.
- the heart—put in the effort required and have a willingness to do the inconvenient things it takes to manifest success.
- the spirit: connect to that within you that matters—the meaning, the purpose, and that which drives your conscience. Your

confidence is strengthened by doing what matters most to your voice and calling.

SWAG comes from knowing you have done the "heavy lifting" needed to be great. You may not know how much heavy lifting you need to do, or may not at first have the discipline you need to see it all the way through to fruition, but this is the path (which goes *through* the opposition) that you need to in order to be great.

You can fool a lot of people but you cannot fool yourself.

Eroding SWAG Enemy No. 4: Tiny or limited thinking and staying inside the box

Every action we take is driven by our thoughts and our thoughts are no wiser than our imagination.

People that stay in "comfort ponds" and always go back to old habits in new ways will never grow their SWAG. When they go to new places or get around more advanced people, they will quickly lose their confidence. They will feel like "fish out of water."

Imagination is seeing the world with the mind's eye. The way you grow your imagination is by carefully feeding your mind, the experiences you choose to participate in, and the education you seek out.

Tiny thinking comes from one place: thoughts of scarcity and limited life.

I remember the first time I left my small town of Woodbury, Tennessee (population 2,500) and went to a university with nearly 23,000 students. I was frustrated and intimidated. I sat in the back of classrooms, tried to fly under the radar, and felt lost and isolated. I acted that way because up until that point in my life I had lived in comfort and security in a place where people knew me. Over time, I began to gain confidence in areas I was interested in but it took years… and I thought I was a person with SWAG!

Here are five key ways you can expand your mindset and overcome the tiny thinking that will limit your bigger future:

1. Try one new thing per week. The thing that scares us the most is usually the one thing we need to do to break through to a bigger life! I've met people who do one thing per day that other people tell them they shouldn't be able to do. The problem is, most of those people are in their 70s! Start early on this one.

2. Experience the world. How could I tell you how beautiful Alaska or Hawaii is if I've never been there? Worldly experiences make you dream bigger and think bigger. Go to two new places each year outside your comfort zone.

3. Get around big thinkers. We become the sum average of the five people we hang around most, and our income will seldom exceed those five people. You may need some new friends! Find people who will challenge you, "stretch" you, and push back when you express limited thinking.

4. Get a mentor who has "been there and done that." A mentor is different than a coach. A coach engages you in a set of systematic and consistent behaviors that allows you to do something tomorrow that you can't do today. A mentor guides and teaches you what to do and what not to do. Make sure your mentor has done what it is you want to do. When I got serious about building my business, I found a mentor who had bought, grown, and sold an enterprise.

5. Remember the saying, "To go beyond your wildest expectations, you first must have some wild expectations." The only thing separating you from others who live grandiose lives is your confidence to try and live it too. Most are not as talented as you and don't have the skill set you have. They just have the SWAG that you don't. Don't you think it's time to expand your horizon?

Eroding SWAG Enemy No. 5: Seeing failure as a person versus an event
Making poor decisions while in transition in life will erode your confidence. How you view rejection in life will also erode your SWAG.

We have all failed. That doesn't make us failures. How we view failure and rejection in life is vital to building, maintaining, and protecting our SWAG. There is no growth without failure. It's a natural step to building your emotional muscles and accumulating wisdom so you can do better in the future.

Maya Angelo, one of the great voices of American literature, said, "When we know better, we do better." Well, we know better by doing and failing!

The next time you fail at anything, put that experience in your "life" suitcase and carry it with you. Be thankful that you tried. Note the progress you made. Chalk it up to poor planning, bad timing, having the wrong people on the bus, bad decisions, scripting from the past, or poor circumstances. Accept responsibility in your own way for the failure.

When it comes to rejection—I'm going to make a bold claim—there is NO rejection in life. Other people may want something different than what we have to offer but they are not rejecting us.

At 25, I went through a terrible breakup with a woman I believed I was supposed to marry. I was devastated and depressed. I was literally sick. My SWAG was non-existent. I searched and searched for the good to come out of that situation and it finally did. I experienced the deepest amount of personal growth and self-reflection during that period—more so than I had at any other point in my life. I became totally self-reliant. I became independent of the "good" opinion of others and made up my mind that my confidence would never be predicated on the views of someone outside of me. I said to myself, "I will never disempower my own self again and allow someone's weakness to control me." This was a breakthrough.

At this same time in my life, a good friend taught me a valuable lesson. She said, "How you are looking at rejection is all wrong. There is no such thing as rejection. She just wants something different than what you have to offer. A different girl will want exactly what you've got."

Today, when you pick one restaurant over another for lunch or dinner, are you rejecting those places? No. You just want something different than what they have to offer. Somebody else will want what they've got. Changing your mindset about rejection will help you shield and protect your SWAG.

Here's the final piece of this transition. When you are in transition in life, something is coming to an end. There is a period of disorientation and confusion and then you experience a re-birth or new beginning. When you are fighting through the recent loss of something, your confidence is low and your past scripting prompts you to go back to old habits in new ways. Because of this, you revert to comfort ponds and are at risk of making bad short-term decisions that can have long-term consequences. This is a dangerous time for your confidence because you will want to go where you feel accepted vs. rejected. You will go to comfort vs. risk. You will go back vs. move forward. Know the three phases of the transition and steel yourself and your SWAG with solid support from people who won't let you make destructive decisions during this period of time. Be open to anything and closed to nothing.

Understand that failure is the cost of doing business. Change the way you see rejection and know the three phases of transition—and how your SWAG factors in to this equation!

Eroding SWAG Enemy No. 6: Being unprepared when opportunity knocks

First off, opportunity doesn't just come knocking. We have to create the environments for it to knock. We do this by sowing the seed, getting ourselves ready, putting ourselves in key situations, doing the heavy lifting, and practicing so that we are ready when it does come.

One thing that erodes SWAG quickly is not being ready and being totally unprepared when there is opportunity to seize. We often chalk this up as bad timing or bad luck but most great people prepare their whole lives for their shot in life and are "all over it" when it finally arrives.

The opposite is for opportunity to land in your lap and finding yourself unable to do anything with it.

This reminds me of a group I knew that through bad financial decisions and poor management were not ready to capitalize on a golden opportunity to capture more market share and strike while the iron was hot. They didn't have any money, and money is exactly what they needed. Because of this, their SWAG was shot. They had no where to go. They felt trapped and isolated vs. confident and focused.

I used a saying while in coaching that sums up this problem; "There comes a time when winter asks what you did all spring and summer." In other words, either you have paid the price or you haven't. Either you have put the time in or you haven't. Either you have made wise decisions or you haven't.

Your SWAG will be eroded if a great opportunity comes and you're simply not ready for it. So how can you prepare? Here are seven attributes people can acquire or develop that will help them build SWAG and avoid being stuck:

1. Knowledge: Work on becoming the go-to market expert. Pay the price in education and learning.

2. Skills: Deliver your knowledge in a way that "blows people's minds." Make the experience with you one that is unforgettable.

3. Effort: Do the inconvenient things it takes to be great. You can't be lazy and still be confident.

4. Likability: Attract people to you by how you make people feel. Help them feel better about themselves when they are with you.

5. Deep Networks: Wake up and get lost in other people's dreams. In turn, they'll want to get lost in yours! You will need deep networks to protect your SWAG when things aren't going well.

6. Connectivity: Be "good for all time zones" so you can connect to people from all walks of life.

7. Free Prize: Know what makes you different and special. It comes from one place—your unique past—meaning your past education, past experiences, past struggles, past mentors, and past scripting.

If you will go to work in these seven areas, you'll increase your SWAG while simultaneously increasing your opportunities. Success will breed more success. Confidence will breed more confidence.

Eroding SWAG Enemy No. 7: Not working our emotional muscles will erode our confidence because in tight places we will fold.

Ever been in a tight place in life and end up making a total failure out of a situation? This happens because of the concept of stimulus and response.

Between what happens to us in life and our response to that stimulus is a space. In that space lies our greatest human freedom—our power to choose how we *respond.*

When we find ourselves in pressure situations and we haven't worked our "emotional muscles," we cave under pressure. This caving looks like blame projected onto other people, a quick readiness to throw in the towel when things get sticky, or an overall lack of resilience to deal with unwanted outcomes or adversity.

In fancy terms, this is called "emotional intelligence," or the ability to bounce back from adversity, be intrinsically self-motivated, "play nice" with others under pressure, and regulate emotions.

Confident people became confident because somewhere along the way they found themselves in tough situations and secured ways to navigate through them without falling apart.

Know this: you will find yourself in high-pressure situations when you play in bigger games in life, get around more confident people, and have to perform to create new and bigger opportunities. You will either be ready or you will not.

Just like you work your physical muscles in the gym, you also need to work your emotional muscles in life situations. We can't see these emotional muscles but we know they are there (or not there!) when the pressure hits. We work these emotional muscles by understanding some key principles:

1. Life is a marathon of starts and stops, ups and downs, successes and failures. Pony up, suck it up, and bounce back when you get knocked down. There is a time and a place where you just have to button your chin strap and fight through the adversity. This builds emotional muscles.

2. **When you go to the gym and have a trainer, he or she engages you in a set of systematic and consistent behaviors over a period of time that allows you to do something tomorrow that you simply cannot do today.** He or she works your muscles many times in preparation for a marathon or whatever endurance test your physical training is targeting. The same concept applies for your emotional muscles and SWAG. Practice over and over and work those muscles constantly, bouncing back from the knock downs so you have the SWAG you need when the real tests come.

3. **There is no transformation of confidence from low-energy thoughts to high-energy thoughts if there is no opposition in life.** It is the opposition that in fact generates the needed, raw emotional material you need to transform your lack of SWAG into an abundance of it. Some people even define confidence as the ability to take obstacles and turn them into opportunities. The obstacles work your emotional muscles, making them stronger.

Do twenty emotional push ups today and thirty tomorrow. One day soon, you will be tested to see if you can do one hundred at one time and you'll be ready.

CHAPTER 3:
BATTLEFIELD PROMOTION

How do we Build SWAG?

Now that we know what erodes our SWAG, let's determine what builds it.

It is not enough to tell people that they have lots of potential and just need more confidence. The true coach and expert teaches people specific ways to understand what confidence really is, what potential really is, and, more importantly, how they might activate it.

In my experiences, people who lack SWAG are *dying* for help in this area but have no idea where to go to get it. Added to that, few people are qualified to break it down and teach them the basics. Remember, part of manifesting your bigger future is having internal assuredness (SWAG) that you can create that which you can envision. Without this, you will always be limited to your current or past results.

In this chapter, I want to break down five big ways you can inspire SWAG in yourself—and ultimately in others. We cannot give away what we don't possess. As we begin to possess more SWAG, others will come to us and want some of it. Sharing it with others will further build our SWAG and serve as a compliment that people want some of what we've got.

We build confidence in five big ways:

1. We step outside our comfort zone and try new things. This involves taking risks, which strengthens our emotional muscles.

2. We "fail forward." This lets us know that failure isn't all that bad and encourages us to "stretch." (What would you do if failure wasn't an option?)

3. We experience mini-victories. These small, incremental steps of success help us build SWAG. Several small victories turn into big victories.

4. We spend time with talent. Being around confident people will help us attain confidence ourselves. We will see them model the behavior we're looking for, and eventually we will see that they accelerate success by the way they respond to various forms of stimuli. We will want some of what they exhibit.

5. We constantly educate ourselves. Experts are confident. They have paid the heavy price of time and hard work to know what they are talking about and position themselves as the go-to people in their industry. Their SWAG attracts people to them because they take complicated things and make them simple.

Let's expand on each SWAG builder so you can add them to your tool kit.

SWAG Builder No. 1: Step outside your comfort zone.

This involves taking risks, which strengthens our emotional muscles. A lack of imagination and only doing what makes you comfortable erodes your SWAG. Confidence comes from trying new things, being exposed to new people and ideas, and opening up your inner dreamer in new and exciting ways.

Many people stay fixed in place in life because they fear the potential outcomes of trying something different or new. Some of the coolest things I've seen in the world only came when I began to travel the world, cultivated a bucket list of places to see, and met interesting people.

If life has become boring, automated, and scripted to you then you need a wake up call. Go ahead and stay a big fish in a small pond if that makes you happy; but there is so much more to the world than just staying put.

You can build SWAG by taking risks in the following small ways that will make a big difference:

• Join an organization you currently don't belong to.
• Get involved in supporting a cause you feel strongly about.

- Pick two places you want to vacation where you've never been before.
- Take a class in a subject area that captures your interest.
- Do one thing per week that you fear.
- Try one new thing this month with your business that you've never tried before.
- Find other people you can teach and mentor in order to share your knowledge.

Each of these exercises will build small doses of SWAG and over time will make you into a more confident person.

C'mon. Take some risks this week! You'll find out that the fear you possess isn't proportionate to the outcome you envision, even in a worst-case scenario.

SWAG Builder No. 2: "Fail Forward"

Fail forward. This lets us know that failure isn't all that bad and encourages us to "stretch."

What would you do with your life if failure wasn't an option? Failing, fear of embarrassment, and worry about what other people will think of you constantly erodes SWAG and shackles people to living exclusively in the glow of their past accomplishments.

Failing forward, by contrast, means you advance confidently in the direction of your dreams and endeavor to live a life that only you can imagine.

Your future is yours. It resides in your imagination. If you let the thought of failure keep you from moving in the direction of that dream, or paralyze you like many people allow to happen, you never attain this important internal knowing that you need to advance your ball down the field.

My first year of being a head coach taught me a lot about failing forward. With a healthy dose of SWAG (back then, many would have called it ego!), I set out to prove how intense I could be as a head coach. I drastically increased the intensity of the program I took over, hell-bent on showing people I was tough and could handle the new assignment.

In this process, four of my five starters were injured. Confident that someone else was to blame for this, I took a trip down to our team doctor to see what the problem was. He said, "Do you really want to know what the problem is?" I said, "Yes I do." He said, "You are the problem. Your increase of the intensity to this level this fast has created the very adversity you are upset about."

Lesson learned. I failed forward with a 13-16 season. The next year, I was determined to change my destiny. To begin the season, we won our first 16 games and were ranked among the top five teams in Tennessee.

Then we became "over confident" when we really hadn't worked our emotional muscles enough to be ready to handle that kind of success. This lead to a false sense of confidence. We would go on to lose seven straight games and digress into a state of pure misery. We finished 18-10, only winning two more games the rest of the season.

What was the end result of this roller coaster ride? Both of these perceived failures (the losing season and the seven-game-losing streak) set us up to win 28 games the next year and from that point forward have seven consecutive twenty-plus win seasons.

We failed. We looked at where we contributed to the failure. We made adjustments and then we moved on. I'm convinced those early struggles are precisely what laid the foundation for a championship almost five years later.

I won't go through the whole Thomas Edison failing 2,000 times before he invented the light bulb story; but most bestselling books I know were turned down by dozens of publishers, including one of my favorite titles, *The Four Hour Work Week* by Timothy Ferris, which became an instant hit globally once published. I've been told "no" by publisher after publisher only to sell thousands of copies of books I wrote that were supposedly "not good enough." Opinions of others don't represent failure, they just represent opinions. Some will buy, some won't buy, so what? Keep on moving. The confidence is in the doing, not in the worrying.

Now get off the couch and start working on some failure! Enough failure will set you up to accelerate your success in the future. I can't tell you how long it will take, but trust me—it's on the way when you're off the bench and in the game.

SWAG Builder No. 3: Experience Mini-Victories

These small, incremental steps of success help us build SWAG. Several small victories turn into big victories.

A mini-victory is a small confidence builder. It's going to the gym when you don't want to go. It's playing nice when you don't feel like it. It's avoiding a pattern that you know creates destructive results in your life. It's self-discipline when you want to be lazy. Private victories precede public victories, and winning the private victory can be tough. But don't be fooled, this is a lot harder than you think.

Sick and tired of being sick and tired one evening after a speaking engagement, I forced myself down to the workout center of a hotel for a workout a little after 9:00 p.m. A few laps on the treadmill while watching the late news, though, and I was done. I hadn't really done anything but waste my time.

That unfulfilling experience led me to a breaking point. I was ready to make my health a top priority. I was finally ready to hire a trainer. I reached out to former Marine and health guru, Rod Key. He said, "I've been waiting on your call. I have the perfect spot for you on Tuesday and Thursday mornings." Without even thinking I said, "I'll take it." He then said it was at 5:00 a.m.

Now, I hadn't been in a gym at 5:00 a.m. in my entire life—but I was committed. Committed to being better. Committed to building the endurance I needed for the road ahead. Committed to building my SWAG.

On my first day of waking up at 4:00 a.m. to get to the gym by 5:00

a.m., I was ready to go. I rolled into the gym and received the first of three gifts from making this tough decision to do something I didn't really want to do.

As soon as I walked in the door, I had the gift of SWAG. I knew I had won my first mini-victory. I got up. I got dressed. I showed up. This was more than 95% of people in the world had done. I looked around and saw all of the successful people working out at 5:00 a.m. (OK, maybe there were a few in there that simply didn't have a life!).

The second gift I received happened on my way home at 6:00 a.m. when I experienced watching the sun come up. Now I had perspective.

When I arrived home, a little confused as to what to do with myself at such an early hour, I remembered my business mentor once telling me to take a "walk of gratitude" in the morning and be thankful for all that I've been fortunate to have and achieve. Now I had three gifts from this one tough decision: SWAG, perspective, and gratitude.

These are "mini-victories." They happen when we make a deposit into our emotional bank accounts, which little by little add up until we build up a reservoir we can call on when needed.

SWAG Builder No. 4: Spend time with talent

This may be a scary thought for some readers: We become the sum average of the five people we hang around the most.

Being around confident people will help us attain SWAG. We will see them model the behavior we're looking for, and eventually we will see that they accelerate success by the way they respond to various forms of stimuli. We will want some of what they've got.

What they have could be summed up in one of these categories:

1. Incredible knowledge: They have paid the price to know their craft.

2. Impeccable skills: They have practiced delivering their knowledge in a way that sparks people to action and elicits buy-in from others.

3. Unmatched effort: They are disciplined in their decision making and approach. Laziness is not in their vocabulary.

4. Internal confidence: They do not allow their SWAG to be stolen by anything or anyone external to them. They *own* their confidence.

5. Deep integrated networks: People of interest are connected. Their support systems elevate them and their brand. They are there in good times and in bad.

6. Universal connectivity: They are good for all time zones relating to those who have and those who don't. They can relate in any audience and play up or play down.

7. Keen awareness of their unique abilities: Confident people know what makes them "unique to the market." It's something that is hard wired and factory installed in them and connected to their platforms or unique past. They compete on this vs. becoming commotitized like most of the world.

In essence, we want what they've got.

Well, here's the good news. Once we know what confident people have, we can begin to acquire these ingredients. My book *Person of Interest- Become the Person Other People Want a Piece of and Can't Live Without* details each of the ingredients in great detail. When you begin to spend time with talent, you see these "intangibles" emerge, and you begin to model the behavior you are looking for.

One of the essential characteristics confident people possess is their resilience, their focused and determined mindsets, and their unique perspectives. My goal is to spend time with talent once per week and more if possible. This can be face to face or by consuming someone's intellectual property, such as their books, CDs, DVDs, or podcasts.

I give the people I coach credit for listening to the podcasts of my radio shows because we regularly have global thought leaders on the show—and I do believe that your radio can become your coach. One hour of feeding your mind positive information can be a game changer for your SWAG. You can replace thoughts of lower-level energy with thoughts of higher-level energy. In the end, that is all spending time with talent is—the transfer of energy. And energy cannot be created, only transferred.

The first step on this cycle is going to workshops, seminars, or YouTube to consume the goods of others. Once you begin to develop your SWAG, you will reach out to others you want to spend time with to pick their brains in person. Of course, they are incredibly busy, as people of interest have packed schedules. You will need to have something to offer them to get on their radar because so many people are vying for their attention, and they only have so much bandwidth to offer.

Go to work on accumulating the seven ingredients in this chapter and you will start being the one that other people want a piece of, which will in turn help build your SWAG.

I have had people tell me that listening to my CDs or podcasts has helped them deal with a divorce, navigate through insecure times in their lives, and help them find their true calling. I regularly consume the work of many great thought leaders in the following ways:

1. I listen to Wayne Dyer, Dan Sullivan, and association industry specific material for speakers and coaches while riding in my car.

2. While getting ready each morning, I keep YouTube Videos of Randy Gage and others playing.

3. When traveling, I watch SharkTank on my iPad to learn more business acumen and negotiating skills.

4. While waiting at restaurants, in drive throughs, or anywhere else, I always have a book in my vehicle.

5. I keep three books loaded on my iPad at all times to consume.

6. I regularly listen to episodes of "Freakanomics" radio.

Building SWAG requires effort. In a global era, there is an overload of videos (see my YouTube Channel at Coach Micheal Burt) and information you can absorb which will better equip you to lead the life of your dreams. All you have to do is make the choice to consume it.

SWAG Builder No. 5: Constantly educate yourself

Experts are confident. They have paid a heavy price to know what they are talking about and position themselves as the go to people in their industry. Their SWAG attracts people to them because they take complicated things and make them simple.

This starts with a mindset that you can learn anything from anybody at any time.

I meet lots of people who are confident in just one thing. They have spent their whole lives cultivating one skill set, but that skill set limits their future potential. In a changing world, we need more than one skill set. We need to be able to solve problems, add value, invent things, seize opportunities, sell something, and build teams. What's the alternative? Your SWAG will be eroded if your one skill set is no longer needed, downsized by technology, or the market changes.

When you constantly educate yourself, you build multiple skills. You become a "must have" vs. a "nice to have."

At some point, every business contract comes up for renewal. At that point, people either need what you have or decide they don't need to depend on the contribution you have made to their lives. People will always need confidence and confident people on their team who can solve problems and take complicated things and make them simple.

Think about the people you seek out in your own life. I bet they are confident. I bet that in your mind they are experts. I bet you admire their skill sets. I bet you consider them to be constant learners and people who are adding value to your life vs. subtracting from it. When you start to become these people, other people will want a piece of what you are offering too. They will want your knowledge. They will want your skills. They will want your mindshare. With a mindset of constant growth and improvement, you will have it to offer.

No matter what industry you are in, if you are trying to become an expert, know this:

- Experts are constantly evolving and learning.
- Experts position themselves in key ways so that the market knows they are the go to people (media, social platforms, events, marketing, books, etc.).
- Experts share brainpower with other experts. They don't replicate, they share and inspire. They are members of mastermind groups, think tanks, and consistent learning mechanisms.
- Experts are hungry. They are never satisfied with past results and are always looking for ways to improve.
- Experts are "critical thinkers." They study, break down, synthesize, and share their "packaged knowledge" with the world.

When you constantly educate yourself, your SWAG will soar because you know you have paid the price to be great. You know you deserve the SWAG you possess.

Experts have what I call the "Big Five" attributes that truly differentiate them from others in the field. These "Big Five" inspire SWAG in the market and ultimately in yourself.

The Big Five are:

1. Great content. Experts say common things in uncommon ways.

2. Great delivery. Experts inspire people to come alive with their knowledge.

3. Great positioning. We know what "lane" they are in, what their expertise is, and what their position is. (Mine is "Everybody needs a Coach in Life.")

4. Great packaging. Their content and brand or personal presentation is packaged in such a way that truly inspires trust in others and tells the market why people should have a relationship with them.

5. Great networks. Constant learners operate in a pond of multipliers. They build the aligned relationships with others who can multiply their dreams and aspirations.

Be open to anything and closed off to nothing. Build SWAG by understanding what drives it up and puts money in your account.

In the next chapter, we learn that SWAG has a big appetite and needs to be fed in order to be protected.

CHAPTER 4:
BATTLE DEFENSE

Protect your SWAG by Feeding It All the Time

We protect our SWAG by "feeding it," and when I say feeding it, I mean feeding it A LOT.

Notre Dame football coach Lou Holtz once said, "What takes years to build up can take seconds to tear down." SWAG can be built, maintained, and protected if you understand each component. Conversely, it can be deconstructed, eroded, and left vulnerable if you don't.

In this chapter, I'll share how to protect your SWAG once you have built it. I'll do so by exploring each of these eight elements:

1. **Body:** eat, sleep, exercise, and paying the price
2. **Mind:** constant engagement
3. **Heart:** deep and meaningful relationships
4. **Spirit:** connectedness to a bigger purpose
5. **Support:** friends who will be there when you need it
6. **Vocation:** finding the distribution channel for your unique talents
7. **Relationships:** people in your life who bring you joy
8. **Rituals:** consistent mechanisms that help you protect your SWAG

SWAG Defender No. 1: Value the body

One of the first things I tell people as it relates to their SWAG is simple: hire a fitness or personal trainer. Nothing will protect the SWAG of your body more, change your eating habits faster, and teach you discipline more effectively than having someone who will push and challenge you as it relates to your body. This is a tremendous confidence builder and protector.

I'm upset now that I didn't hire one sooner in life. I did not work out in the past as hard as I do now that I have a coach pushing me.

Whatever phobia you have about getting into gyms, exercising in front of other people, working out with a trainer, or any other excuse, get rid of it. This will be a game changer for you.

There are three simple ways to protect the SWAG of the body:
1. Eat right.
2. Sleep right.
3. Exercise.

Whatever diet you choose, stick with it. I frequently go on low-sugar diets as a way to be healthier. This is difficult, and you need an accountability partner. However, there is nothing better than feeling healthy and in shape. It builds and protects your SWAG.

Sleeping right involves establishing patterns, getting ample rest, and achieving deep sleep. If you burn the candle at both ends by getting up early and staying up late, your SWAG and your diet will suffer. My SWAG is always higher when I'm in bed early. Plus, there's some kind of adrenaline rush about knowing you are getting great sleep.

Exercise does not mean walking in your subdivision. This will not protect your SWAG. What protects your SWAG is knowing that you have paid the price, you have pushed yourself to new limits, and that you really worked out. Going half-way through a modified workout will not protect SWAG, it will erode it. Once you get your trainer, you will see a new level of commitment and sacrifice. This will feed your SWAG.

One more thing: do your workouts at 5 or 6 o'clock in the morning. The mini-victories of getting up, showing up, and sweating before 95% of the world is even out of bed will drive your SWAG through the roof. You'll feel like a million bucks and be confident enough to tackle whatever life throws at you that day.

This is simple, but powerful—eat right, sleep right, exercise right. Your SWAG will explode!

SWAG Defender No. 2: Engage the mind

The mind is like a muscle. The more you work it, the stronger it gets. Consider that at 99 years old, the great UCLA basketball coach John Wooden was meeting with people, writing books, and totally engaged.

People who are not confident don't exercise their minds. They are stuck in the past, stuck in tiny and limited thinking, and stuck repeating the same old tired patterns over and over.

Early in my life, I was turned on to learning and began to make learning a way of being. It became part of the very fabric of my life. I always have a book, CD, podcast, video, or something with me. Knowledge is a SWAG builder. Being in the dark on trends, ideas, or current happenings decays SWAG because you just can't fake it when you don't know what you are talking about.

The decision to engage your mind in an ongoing, consistent manner is a personal one. No one can make you do it. I suggest finding someone that you "emotionally identify" with and begin to study their work. Watch their videos, read their books, and consume their goods. Become a disciple of their work. Do the heavy lifting to become an expert in your field. Once you pay the price, you'll begin to build your SWAG. You'll want to speak up and be involved in conversation, in local happenings, in industry functions. Others will affirm and validate your confidence because they will turn to you to have solutions to their challenges. You'll begin to transform their low energy to high energy and in the process you'll be transformed as well.

You will become the go-to person in your industry because you have paid the mental price to be great. Others will detect this and climb on board your band wagon.

SWAG Defender No. 3: Ignite the heart

I used to define passion as "the irresistible belief for motive or action." I now say "that which excites."

Passion is the total engagement of the heart. It's being "all in" with something. It's being willing to do the inconvenient things it takes to be great. It's being involved with things that bring tremendous joy to our lives.

You show me a person who doesn't have passion for what they are involved in, and I'll show you a person lacking in SWAG. They either don't have the confidence to get off the bus and navigate into uncertain waters or don't have the confidence to put their whole selves into what they are doing.

When we pay the price with effort and passion, we know we deserve the fruits of our labor. It builds our SWAG. We deserve success—we know it deep down in our core.

The opposite is true when we have not paid the price. We are not confident. We are merely obligated to something that we don't want to be obligated to; therefore, *we put part of ourselves in as if we are playing the hokey pokey.*

When the heart is not involved, you will only be mediocre; and when you put forth mediocre value to the world, it rewards you with mediocre rewards. Only the best receive the big-time recognition, referrals, repute, and money. Only those who guard their hearts and passion play under the lights. Make a decision today that you will be "all in" or "all out." Living a life anywhere in between those extremes will erode your SWAG.

You can fool lots of people lots of the time but you can never fool yourself. You know if you are engaged or not. Find things you can be totally engaged in by asking these four questions:

1. What do I love doing?
2. What am I great at doing?
3. What fills my heart with good feelings when I'm doing it?
4. How can I take what I love and what I'm good at and make money doing it?

Answer these four questions and you're on your way to igniting your heart.

It may seem like everyone in the world uses the word passion, but it's so vital to every equation. It's the fuel, the energy, and the ammunition to really be great. It's what we have on the inside that we transfer to others that people can feel. It turns people on versus turns them off.

One day after a speaking engagement, I walked out of the venue and told my team, "I never thought I would see the day that people would pay for passion packaged but it's here." People are yearning for passion that is packaged in a way that they can take with them to ignite the seeds in their lives.

Confident people play to the hilt. They leave it all on the court. They don't hold anything back. These people lead with the heart.

SWAG Defender No. 4: Feed our spirit

Spiritual intelligence drives all other intelligences.

Some believe that conscience is God's voice to his children. When we fall out of alignment with the one who created us, we lose our confidence. We begin to make poor decisions that contradict our internal voice of right and wrong. Because of our lack of internal confidence, we cave in when there is pressure leading us away from our creator and into destructive waters. In essence, it's a selfish thing. We look out for what is best for us versus what is best for those we are involved with.

We can feed our confidence with the following spiritual things to keep us in alignment with our source:

- daily meditation and prayer;
- daily reading of spiritual literature;
- time spent in nature admiring God's work and letting it inspire us;
- surrounding ourselves with spiritual people;
- regularly attending spiritual practices such as church, small groups, and events;
- having a spiritual coach in our lives with whom we can discuss our struggles and who serves as a spiritual mentor to us.

In a world that pushes us in the other direction and leads us to believe that success is built on material things, we need to bring more enlightenment into our lives. Constantly assessing what are the most important things in your life by taking regular and consistent breaks in nature will slow you down and help you get back in alignment with your source. Your confidence will rise when you make and keep commitments to yourself in these areas and discipline yourself to stay away from destructive habits stemming from short-term decision making that could have long-term consequences.

This may be one of the single greatest ways to protect your SWAG—and the most important. Cultivating a personal relationship with the big man upstairs will build an inner knowing that whatever you are experiencing in life is part of a greater plan.

One of my favorite scriptures is Jeremiah 29:11 where the Lord says, "I have plans for you. Plans to prosper you and not to harm you."

Ask yourself, "What is my plan and how can I go and execute it?"

SWAG Defender No. 5: Through the support systems we cultivate

Everyone needs support—support when we fail; support when we succeed; support when we are confused; support when we have low energy and low confidence; support when we are in transition; and support just to work through ideas we have in our minds to reassure us we are doing the right thing.

A good support system is a "transformation system." You will go to them with a lack of clarity, lack of confidence, and insecurity about your future, and because of their knowledge, skills, desire, and SWAG, they will transform you.

I meet lots of people who have no support systems. It's just them and a few people they interact with every day. They have no mentors, no leaders, and no support. Because of this, when they encounter challenges—as we all do—they have no one to turn to.

Many times, these scant few advisors a person does have in their life are way too close to the situation to offer solid advice and counsel. This also limits your idea pool. We need new ideas, new content, and fresh ways of looking at old problems. These support systems could come in the form of a personal board of advisors or directors, great friends, mentors who have "been there and done that," or associations and groups who are facing similar things.

As you know, I believe that "Everybody needs a Coach in Life." A great coach will do three important things for you:

1. Make you have conversations you don't want to have;
2. Push you to do things you may not want to do;
3. Help you become something you didn't even think you could become.

In my bestselling book *This Ain't No Practice Life*, I mentioned the need for a "personal board of directors." In essence, this is your "dream team" that will advance your dream down the field toward your dominant aspiration. Trust me, you need these people. No big accomplishment in life was ever attained through rugged individualism. It takes a village to raise a person.

My personal board of directors looks like this:

1. a business mentor
2. a spiritual mentor
3. a board of advisors
4. two or three great friends I speak to daily
5. a significant other
6. my immediate family (in my opinion, a family is a feeling and doesn't have to be a blood line)
7. associations you belong to that promote what you do
8. a strategic coaching program (strategiccoach.com)

I suggest you meet with your personal board of directors at least quarterly, and some will come in handy more often than that during certain seasons of your life. You are just one person away from a whole new season in your life because if the right person walks into your life, he or she can completely change the season.

Here's my challenge to you. Be a "Go-Giver" (Burg) and get lost in other people's dreams. This will endear people to you, and when you ask for help, they will be there with bells on to help you.

SWAG Defender No. 6: See work as the distribution channel for our talents

You can see your work in one of two ways:

1. As an OCCUPATION to you, that which occupies your time and energy, and for which you receive a paycheck. You're there with the body but not there with the most important parts of your being—your mind, heart, and spirit. This is just work to you.

2. As a VOCATION, which stems from the Latin term meaning voice, or calling in life. In this setting, you see work as the distribution channel for your unique talents. You are no longer trading your time and energy for money but rather trading your passion and your talents for purpose. Money follows you all the way to the bank. In this setting, you are "all in" with your body, your mind, your heart, and your spirit. You no longer need external motivation because it is intrinsic. You are on the right bus in life, you distribute your talents through your work, and the world rewards you in meaningful ways with money, love, referrals, reputation, and recognition.

I've never met a confident person who was on the wrong bus in life. By contrast, people with no SWAG struggle through work. They dread work. They merely "survive" their work weeks, and pursue their passions off the job.

Confident people create their work. Confident people see their work as their true calling. They give their heart and soul to their calling. They are self-disciplined and know that much of their legacy in life will be directly tied to their distribution channel for their work and how many people they can directly impact.

We protect our SWAG by using this opportunity to find our calling vs. find a job. This is another area where our education system drastically under prepares people for their bigger futures. We don't have classes in finding our calling. We have classes in curriculum and subject matter, but we don't have classes in finding the right bus for our lives.

Almost all of us find our calling in life by being turned on to something by somebody.

At six years old, a little league baseball coach affirmed in me that I would become a coach someday, and that affirmation gave me confidence. That confidence was then affirmed further by other coaches, teachers, and mentors who also gave me opportunity and opened doors for me.

Until you find the right work for you, de-motivation and a lack of SWAG will continue to haunt you. Your own conscience will tell you that you have more to offer, and every time it does it will either motivate you to move in the direction of your dreams or will take another chip out of your SWAG.

Take any superstar that you pay hundreds of dollars to watch at a concert or a ballgame. Do you believe someone has to drag them out of bed and encourage them to get up on that stage or on that ball field and entertain tens of thousands of screaming fans who are rewarding them with attention, love, energy, and money? You are paying to watch them work! Their work just happens to be their vocation, their calling, their love!

Protect your SWAG by finding your calling. If you need help, pick up a copy of *This Ain't No Practice Life* where I discuss seven important decisions to finding your voice in life. Once you find it, coupled with your unique abilities and talents, you will be off to the races.

Your SWAG will go through the roof!

SWAG Defender No. 7: Feed our relationships

Healthy relationships with others help us protect our SWAG. I've seen people who can't move into the future because of their past relationships with various people.

As we begin to mature, we accept people for who they are and what they are able to give at certain times in their lives. We abandon judgment.

We adopt forgiveness. We see beyond whatever transgressions have happened to us and we extend grace as grace has been extended to us. Like an unopened birthday gift, we open up grace and try and understand why people do what they do vs. what they did.

No other show I've ever recorded impacted my life greater than the two shows I did on The Power of Forgiveness. Simply put, we drop the ball in life. We transgress against others. We make mistakes and we come up short. Just as we want grace and forgiveness extended to us, we too should extend this to others. This helps us get out of the mental prisons of the past and create positive emotional space for the future.

During my radio show, motivational speaker, bestselling author, and television personality Larry Winget once said, "Two halves don't make a whole when it comes to relationships." He said, "Two wholes, who are well adjusted whole people, make a whole."

Relationships are the core of our existence. They deeply affect our mindsets, our emotions, and our energy. When we are in destructive, low-energy relationships, it deteriorates our energy. It drains us of possibilities. It holds our futures hostage.

Too many people allow others to control their SWAG, especially their relationships. I've seen good people who possess lots of potential get involved with the wrong people and have their lives ruined in a very short period of time. Their weaknesses allowed another to manipulate and control them and destroy their SWAG.

No other person can control your SWAG—not your parents, your spouse, friends, co-workers, or children. We have to work to cultivate healthy relationships with people who value us. There is a value-for-value transaction.

We do become the sum average of the five people we hang around the most. Some suggest that our income will seldom exceed the five people we hang around the most. Who we associate with and what relationships we enter into either propel us toward our bigger futures or limit our bigger futures.

Protect your SWAG by really thinking about your choices and spending time with people who add value to your life, and you to theirs. See the good in people. Build people up vs. tear them down. Seek first to understand and then to be understood. Be a "Go-Giver" vs. a "Go-taker."

Protect the "special" within your relationships and you'll protect your SWAG.

SWAG Defender No. 8: Create rituals that we can live by

I'm not sure anyone had more rituals than I did when I was coaching. Some called it borderline superstition, but the bottom line is that when I practiced my "rituals" I felt more confident. I had practice day rituals, game day rituals, outfit rituals, and more. A ritual is just a practice that helps you build your SWAG.

When I speak now, I try and get in a room prior to the engagement and breathe deeply, relax, and visualize the audience being connected to my message. Before a sales presentation, I visualize the economic buyers saying "yes" to what I'm offering.

I workout with a trainer every Tuesday and Thursday at 5:00 a.m. This too is a ritual, and rituals practiced consistently will protect your SWAG. The opposite is to be all over the place with no rhythm or plan and to go into situations with low confidence.

A ritual builds rhythm and SWAG. Not long ago, I hosted Michael Maher on my radio show. He has positioned himself as the "most referred real estate agent in the country." He had a ritual for everything that included a pre-bed ritual, an early-morning ritual, and an end-of-day ritual. This helped him build, maintain, and protect his SWAG.

I have a Sunday ritual of planning my week around the highest use of my time so that once I get into the week I can execute. I have a ritual of touching base with three of my biggest advocates per week in a meaningful way.

Businessman, motivational speaker, and college president Dr. Nido Qubein has a ritual of writing four personal letters and making four phone calls per day. These are all rituals that build consistency and focus into your life.

Here are some simple rituals I use to protect my SWAG:
1. I plan my week on Sunday for 20-40 minutes.
2. I work out with a trainer twice per week for one hour beginning at 5:00 a.m.
3. I watch videos of *Shark Tank* while on planes traveling to increase my business acumen.
4. I listen to motivational CD's while in the car, creating a "rolling university."
5. I take a three-to-six day "mini-retirement" for every 60 days of work in order to rejuvenate.
6. I eat breakfast with one of my best friends every Saturday morning.
7. I take notes on my iPad for new blogs I want to write.

If you want to protect your SWAG, you will begin to build some consistency, focus, and rhythm into your life.

Now that we have protected the confidence of our lives, we must shift to protecting the confidence of our business. In the next chapter, I share three powerful ways to protect the SWAG of your business so you never have to worry about the up and down cycles many business owners experience.

CHAPTER 5:
THE BATTLE OUT THERE

Protect the SWAG of Your Business

There are several ways that we protect the SWAG of our business. These are about mindset and motivation because once you lose these two things, your sales will drop, your morale will drop, and your business can go quickly into a death spiral.

Remember, SWAG is the one thing that affects everything, and once it's lost it's hard to get back.

We've seen what consumer confidence can do to an economy. Once people lose faith in you and your services, your referrals will dry up and your business will decline. It's just that simple. On the other hand, when you build, maintain, and protect your personal SWAG, your business SWAG will swell. People will notice. Others will be attracted to you and what you have to offer.

The *three key* ways you can protect the SWAG of your business are:

1. Never use "outside indicators" to determine your sense of self-worth.
2. Commit to total engagement in your business in a consistent and systematic manner.
3. Use the "peace of mind quadrant" that utilizes five key areas to measure at all times.

Let's explore these in greater detail.

Never using "outside indicators" to determine your sense of self-worth.

Just as your personal SWAG is never predicated by anything or anyone outside of you, neither is the SWAG of your business. The first time you use words like "economy," "recession," or "seasons of the year," you are in trouble.

I coach a lot of real estate agents, and sometimes they are the world's worst about letting outside factors affect their SWAG. I remind them that the top agents I coach never allow the economy to affect their efforts or their values. Top agents always reach their goals, regardless of what the economy is doing. Your sales in your business are determined by and proportionate to the value you create to the market.

This is a good time for the lesson of self-appraisal vs. market value. The market never lies. If you don't have the sales that you think you should, it is a strong indication that the product or service you are putting out there is simply not good enough. You need to turn the focus back on to you, your product, or your service.

The market buys that which is good. Just take note of the billions of dollars being spent on solutions to problems people have all over the world. Some people self-appraise themselves much higher than their true market value, and because of this, their SWAG is shot. If you are struggling in your business, stop the whining, stop the projecting, stop the finger pointing, and ask a hard question: How attractive is your business to the market?

Randy Gage, a former high school dropout who rose from a jail cell as a teen to become a self-made multi-millionaire, once said there are two ways to make money: solve problems and create value. Do both and you get rich. The bigger the problem and the bigger the solution, the bigger the payout. When you start getting into a mindset that customers should just show up because you opened the doors (and you think you are great), you are in deep trouble.

Add value. Open the doors. Market and advertise. Expose people to your business. Quit waiting on people to just show up because you went into business. This is a reactive way to live and one in which your SWAG will always be predicated on external factors.

Another popular place some people put their confidence is in the outcomes of elections. I started my business in the middle of a recession, was selling an intangible, and still found a way to show a profit based on pure effort and SWAG.

I hire people in recessions. I buy land in recessions. I take risks in recessions because my SWAG is never predicated by anything outside of myself.

My sales are predicated on how much we work to "circulate with purpose" and how active we are at making sure the people we want to do business with know how we can help them. We look for big problems to solve, niches we can own, and ways we can create tremendous value for the world so that people need us in their lives. We want to become "must haves" vs. "nice to haves." If you are a "nice to have," then your days are numbered.

Focus on what you can control, which is you. Your SWAG is protected when you have a plan, when you are measuring key things that point to truths about your business, and when you are moving with purpose.

Your SWAG will be destroyed if you wake up and hope somebody will show up. It's not happening. Go out there and create SWAG by getting into the game!

Total engagement in your business in a consistent and systematic manner.

SWAG is destroyed when you are not engaged in life. If you're not engaged in relationships, you will have no long-term confidence that it will last.

Likewise, one way to protect the SWAG of your business is total engagement in a systematic and coordinated manner. Weekly involvement with key decision makers, getting to know your people's hot buttons, measuring key performance indicators, and staying current on the trends and markets in which you operate all serve to build and protect your SWAG.

I've coached lots of people who have become disengaged from their business because of these reasons:

1. **Personal life** (They fell prey to circumstances ranging from divorce to addiction to depression.)
2. **Boredom** (They excelled at the pinnacle of their career but are now

bored with doing the same thing over and over.)

3. **Burnout** (They ran too hard for too long and are now operating in mechanical or burn out mode.)

4. **Abdication** (They turned their business over to ill-informed or incompetent people who decay the values of the business.)

5. **Lack of focus** (They got too interested in too many different things at the expense of being great at one thing.)

6. **Multi-tasking** (They created too many things to focus on at one time causing information overload.)

7. **Undisciplined** (They were dreamers and not grinders who had great ideas but did not have the substance to see their ideas through to their logical conclusion.)

When you become disengaged in your business, you lose focus, desire, and SWAG. To regain it, you must get back in the trenches and pay attention to the little things, because the little things are actually the big things.

Here are some ways you can protect your SWAG by being fully engaged in your business:

- See your work as the *distribution channel* for your talents that the world rewards with love, money, recognition, and referrals.
- Prepare your monthly intentions and share them with your team at the beginning of each month. These should be no more than seven things you are going to manifest, study, or share with your team in a 30-day window. At the end of each month, do a full report to the team on what you actually did.
- Use a *scoreboard* that tracks the important activity toward the company's dominant focus and get reports weekly on both activities and results. Have set times that these are turned in and accept no excuses. This forces people to plan their weeks, which is where manifestation and intention begins.
- Have your team share their weekly intentions at the beginning of each week. See that they are in alignment with your best customer—getting

strategies to determine the synergy between each group. Use a vision board (www.coachburt.com) to convey lead indicators of what the group will be doing each week to attract customers to the business.

- Do a mid-week education session on one key concept to grow the knowledge, skills, desire, and SWAG of your group by sharing what you have with them.
- Perform an end-of-week autopsy to determine what worked, what didn't, and what your strategy is for the next week. This should be at a consistent time so expectations are set.
- Make a personal trip to see four gurus per year who will "sharpen your saw" and re-engage you when you lose your fire. Spending time with talent always motivates and inspires.

When you are truly engaged in anything you do, your SWAG is naturally going to elevate. It's perfectly normal to become overwhelmed and want to shut it down or to abdicate responsibility to others for your business. However, this is a short-term solution to a long-term problem. Once you have impeccable systems and people in place, you can continue to delegate and potentially just own your business. Until then, engagement is necessary for your growth and sustainability.

Use the peace of mind quadrant.

One day it came to me that what people really want is peace of mind and some important freedoms in life. I call this the peace of mind quadrant, which is premised on five key freedoms.

The peace of mind quadrant begins with a dominant focus—a tangible outcome you would like to obtain in a twelve-month cycle and which is measured in 30-day units. Once you know this, you know what your championship is to win and where all of your energy should be devoted.

You then need a strategy or multiple mechanisms to drive you toward this dominant focus. This could be your marketing and advertising plan coupled with your personal lead generation cycle and the various methodologies you will be using to attain the dominant focus.

You want to hit your dominant focus consistently because when you do this, it offers the owner/entrepreneur five emotional freedoms. Along the way, you're going to want the peace of mind that what you are doing is working. Knowing important areas of your business builds SWAG and helps to protect your confidence.

Pilots tell us that out of all the instruments they use to ensure their plane gets from point A to point B, there are really only five key dials that help them navigate. All the other dials merely support the five key instruments. In your business, there five important things that need to be measured at all times, and when you have an awareness of these five key areas, you have one big thing: SWAG. SWAG to make decisions. SWAG to expand into new markets. SWAG to hire new people, and SWAG that what you are doing is working or not working. The opposite is a guessing game where you don't know what is working and what is not.

Here are the five important dials we watch in my business:

1. Weekly/Monthly sales. Where are we in relationship to our weekly and monthly goals? These reports are generated by Friday at 2:00 p.m.

2. Activity toward goals. We believe results always follow the right activity. We measure our high-value activities toward our goals and dial up or down depending on what our sales numbers represent.

3. Run way money. This is expected or delivered money vs. collected money. This tells us how much money we have and what we will see in the coming months.

4. Pipeline. This dial measures those in our "farm club" who are legitimate prospects and who are interested in our business.

5. Love for current customers. We call these net promoters or those who are actively referring us to other people. At all times, I want to know what we are doing to love our customers in meaningful ways.

These five dials help us protect the SWAG of our business because they tell us where we are and what we need to be doing.

Once you have your dominant aspiration in place and you have a strategy to reach your aspirations (coupled with your measurement tools), you will begin to build the five key freedoms into your life, which include:

1. Money freedom—All your future days are paid for.

2. Time freedom—You can work from anywhere at any time and are not shackled by the restraints of a job working for someone else.

3. Physical freedom—You have valuable time to work on you and protect the great asset of your body.

4. Spiritual freedom—You make important time each week to connect with your creator and connect with your highest self.

5. Ultimate freedom—There are no limitations on your life.

Your dominant aspiration = a focus for your energy. Your selling mechanisms = a customer acquisition strategy to build wealth. Your five dials = a measurement tool to track and measure important areas of your business. Your five key freedoms = what you get when you get to the top.

Acquisition of the five "emotional freedoms" is the number one reason we start or grow our own business. Instead of working years to build something you don't own and cannot sell, we go to work on our own business to "buy" us these emotional freedoms.

A business should be designed so that it serves your life, not runs your life. Always remember that "a business is designed before there is a business."

CHAPTER 6:
THE BATTLE WITHIN
The difference between SWAG, arrogance, and boldness

I've got a good friend who is in real estate. One day he said to me, "There's a difference between self-appraisal and market value."

Just like some self-appraise their house much higher than the market will pay for it, some also give themselves a much higher appraisal in the market than the market value can command. This can lead to arrogance, or inflated self-importance.

Some mistake SWAG for arrogance; but that is usually only those who are insecure or not very confident in themselves.

For the purposes of this book, I define all three as:

1. Confidence - The memory of success and the internal knowing that one can create or manifest that which they envision in life.

2. Boldness - Strategies or tactics to stand out and look different than others to capture the attention of a desired group or market.

3. Arrogance - Inflated self-importance. Self-appraisal is much higher than market value.

Many times, this is all in the eyes of the beholder. A confident person can be bold to grab the attention of the market as it relates to differentiation. This is a necessary step in today's saturated world.

Sometimes the confident person becomes arrogant. Characteristics of this would be snubbing other people, a constant state of judgment of others, or an overall disposition that one is simply better than others. We want to be confident and bold, not confident and arrogant.

If you practice the concepts in this book, you will be able to build, maintain, and protect your greatest asset—SWAG. You will know what erodes it and also how you can regenerate it once it is lost.

I believe SWAG is the great enabler or the great disabler of success, and it's so disheartening to see so many talented people under achieve and have unrealized potential because they are essentially holding themselves back.

You don't have to be one of these people. Although this subject is never taught in school, it is a "must-have" characteristic if one is to achieve long-term success and happiness in life.

It's this simple. SWAG is the one thing that affects everything. For some, SWAG appears to be hardwired into them. It's almost as if God put the special ingredient of a confident mind and heart in some while others have to work harder to acquire this elusive trait.

I believe SWAG can be built, maintained, and protected. When eroded, I believe it can be re-captured.

For too long, parents have said to their children, "You have loads of potential. You just need more confidence." With no classes or instruction in confidence, this only confuses the child as they know they lack this special ingredient but can't seem to find it anywhere. We must understand confidence or SWAG as the "X factor," the one thing that propels people into a new and bigger arena.

This book is about going to work tackling the complex and making it simple. It's about going to work on a deeper level of exploring something that affects all 7.5 billion people on planet Earth. If you don't acquire this ingredient of SWAG somewhere along your journey, your dreams will go unfulfilled and you will live a reactive life vs. a proactive one. You will live by default vs. by design.

With SWAG, by comparison, nothing is out of the realm of possibility for you. You will dramatically increase the probability of accomplishing that which you envision in your mind.

I wish you the best of luck on the journey. You have the seeds of greatness inside you!

ABOUT THE AUTHOR

Micheal Burt is a self-described "coachepreneur," a new blend of focus and intensity with an entrepreneurial mind and a coaching acumen.

By starting coaching at age 15 and spending his first decade of his professional life winning championships as a head basketball coach, Burt infuses business principles into the athletic world and athletic principles into the business world in a way that moves people and produces serious results. This blend positions him as the go-to expert in the country with a unique ability to coach groups and individuals toward some big dominant focus in their lives, taking the complicated and making it simple. Burt has spent his life studying confidence, or what he likes to call SWAG, learning how to build it, what erodes it, and how to protect it.

Coach Burt has been hired by some of the biggest brands in the world to "coach up" their people. These brands have included Dell, Inc., State Farm Insurance, National Health Care, Vanderbilt University, The National Home Builders Association, and more.

Coach Burt is also the host of *Change Your Life Radio* on the FoxNews Affiliate in Nashville, Tennessee. He spends time with some of the top thought leaders in the country. Go to www.coachburt.com to listen to past podcasts.

SWAG is Coach Burt's tenth book. To date, he has sold more than 50,000 copies of his books. Burt also speaks more than 150 times nationally per year and practices what he preaches by coaching teams of people toward a dominant focus in their lives on a regular basis as a real practitioner.

Micheal Burt Enterprises, LLC is a firm that specializes in coaching and developing the talent in organizations. Specifically, the company helps create "monster growth" in individuals and organizations who drive the new American dream. It does this through speaking, coaching, training, leading, radio, resources, products, and corporate memberships.

Learn more about Coach Burt and what Micheal Burt Enterprises, LLC can do for you at www.coachburt.com.

Listen to Coach Burt on *Change Your Life Radio* every Sunday from 2-3 p.m. CST globally at www.iheart.com (Click on WLAC) as he tackles universal challenges like confidence, forgiveness, business growth, team building, and living a remarkable life. Podcasts are available by searching Coach Micheal Burt on iTunes.